LIVES DISCOLORED

LIVES DISCOLORED

How Paul Was Lost to Drugs

ALUNEY ELFERR

authorHOUSE®

AuthorHouse™
1663 Liberty Drive
Bloomington, IN 47403
www.authorhouse.com
Phone: 1-800-839-8640

Cover: Aluney Elferr
2nd edition
1st printing
(2012)

Published by AuthorHouse   01/26/2013

ISBN: 978-1-4817-0087-0 (sc)
ISBN: 978-1-4817-0086-3 (e)

Library of Congress Control Number: 2012923873

CONTENTS

I dedicate this work, first to the Lord's Vineyard, God, for without Him nothing exists.
To my parents, Aluysio and Liney, from whom I inherited everything.
To my wife and eternal love Suely Brazil, who taught and showed me happiness.
To my children, Aluney Junior, Laura Elferr, and Maria Clara, who total and sublimate my being.
To all the friends and supporters of this cause and all the sons and daughters who are on drugs and suffering immensely and to their ability to discover their paths with a single north—*happiness.*

LIVE LIKE THE FLOWERS

"Master, how do I not bother?
Some people talk too much; others are ignorant.
Some are indifferent.
I hate those who are liars.
I resent those who slander."

"Live like flowers!" warned the master.

"How do I live like the flowers?" asked the disciple.

"Look on these flowers," continued the master, pointing to the lilies that grew in the garden. "They are born in the manure, but they are pure and fragrant. They extract smelly compost to grow and are useful and healthy but do not let the bitterness of earth stick to the freshness of their petals. It is fair to agonize with one's own sins, but it is not wise to allow the vices of the other to inconvenience you. Their defects are theirs and not yours. If they're not your own, there is no reason to bother with them. Exercise, therefore, the virtue of rejecting all evil that comes from outside. This is to live like flowers."

About the Book

The book tells the story of a drug user and all he did to resist drugs when his friends first offered them at a young age. But he didn't resist, and the story tells of the suffering and the sorrows that resulted and all that his family faced to see him out of this.

But leaving drugs is not so easy, and the story shows the parallel universe that is involved in all of this.

We can learn also that we must stay far away from this life of drugs because the sorrow is too large, and it will keep us away from happiness.

All teachers and parents should read this in order to learn to see clearly what our society tries over and over to ignore.

This is a story of overcoming that will make you breathe deeply and think about all those people in the world who are living dead—whose only thought is of the next fix, the next gulp, the next breath of death.

The narrator of *Lives Discolored* begins, "I've always been a normal person, I believe. I had a good childhood, and my parents were always present, or at least they were as far back as I remember. I lived with my parents, attending school and sometimes church. Sometimes, I fooled around, just like every kid in the world. And until I was fifteen, I had, I think, a very nice life.

He continues, "But this is my life story, a story that I find fascinating. And I hope all who read it will reflect on their lives. For this, I spent twelve hours writing. I wrote the story of my life. And the love showed here is the love of God for you all.

"One day, we will find ourselves up!"

INTRODUCTION

I've always been a normal person, I believe. I had a good childhood, and my parents were always present, or at least they were as far as I remember. I lived with my parents, attending school and sometimes church. Sometimes I fooled around, just like every kid in the world. And until I was fifteen, I had, I think, a very nice life.

I also had some friends in my childhood. But things began to change, and the unknown was coming.

But this is my life story, a story that I find fascinating. And I hope all who read it will reflect on their lives. For this I spent twelve hours writing. I wrote the story of my life. And the love showed here is the love of God for you all.

One day, we will find ourselves up!

Live happy!

DAYS LITTLE COLORED

God's Mill Grinds Slow but Sure

THE MEETING

It was another day like any other—a morning without much to do. In fact, I used to always wake up at noon, and after eating something, I'd wander around the house, seeing things in black and white; you know, it seemed that nothing was rational. My life seemed to make no sense; I felt useless sometimes, with a huge, hollow hole inside me. I was bewildered for no reason.

It was not always so. Until I was fifteen, I lived a pretty good life. My relationship with my parents was close and enjoyable. I attended good schools and got good grades. On several occasions, I became the number one student.

I used to have faith, or at least I frequented my church very often. I did not understand everything there, but I tried to follow my parents, who always took me to pray in the church and made me look good; and I did not even notice the importance of religion in my life.

As time went on, as happens to anyone, I sometimes met friends at school. I called them friends because I really thought they were friends. And these friends always told me they wanted to present to me a real life, a better and more "happy" life. They were encouraging me to take drugs with them, and this stuff was called a better life.

Wow, taking drugs was really not something better; it was dumb stuff. It would probably make you feel a little dizzy, and soon after, the hell would come to your head. I did not really understand what taking drugs involved, since my life was good. But we always tend to believe these guys, don't we?

Why did I need a better life?

Several times, I thought I would find the happier "life" that "friends" offered me with some frequency in school and sometimes even after church, which should never happen. But such is the human being. We always want more, and seeking this "always more" often ends up badly for the seeker.

Time passed, and I always took as a joke Carlos and Antonio's proposals. Carlos and Antonio were two of my closest friends. They claimed to have a better life than I had. They were selling an idea, but in reality, things were the other way around. I mean, they were turning a better life into a worse life, a life of grief.

The market for drugs is always good, just like that for cigars and beers. You never see ugly people or sick people smoking cigars and drinking beers on TV commercials. Rather, you see beautiful women and men. Drugs are like that.

I always sought to speak with my father about most things that happened to me. And often, Daddy guided me. But when it came to the doubts that I had about this "good life," he seemed not to care much. When I repeatedly asked him about this life or said that friends were offering me a happiness I never knew, my father played and said, "Son, whatever anyone chooses to accept for himself is a better life."

Today I know that Dad could have been more careful with his answer.

But back to that time; I accepted my friends offer. I made my mind up and started taking drugs. That was the beginning of the tragedy. In that moment, I did not realize how stupid a decision that was. I would only realize that years later.

Most of these friends who I met through this "better life" had begun using because of the same promise that they were offering me!

It was then that I went with them. I accepted their invitation, and we had a "meeting" right after school. At least I thought it was a meeting, but it was nothing. We sat in the bushes very close to school. Antonio, always alert, kept looking all around.

"What is this wonderful life that can only be seen by us?" I asked. I did not understand why my friend was so worried about people passing by.

That was when I had the first accurate information. Anthony said, "Be cool; the 'stuff' cannot be seen in our hands, and no one can smell it.

But wait, I thought. *What kind of life is this?* I wondered.

Antonio took several sacks from his pocket and began to put the contents of his bag on a school board. He covered his nostril and sniffed with the other what he called "the little path." But how could some white powder give a better life?

I was there and could not back out, both because I would have been ashamed and because I wanted to try the stuff. It was cocaine, the very first drug I'd ever taken. What can a man do? He sniffs such a powder, and he thinks he is the best.

Well, I tried. I felt something I'd never before felt in my life. I saw things I had never seen. I saw the stars very close to me; it seemed I was taking a trip into space or something like that. The time was relaxing; I had no sense of the moment. I snorted the drug, though I'm not sure how many of the little paths I used. The only thing I knew was that I was the last to leave the bushes. I really was the last to leave the place where I first met the killer, the murderer of my days. I was flanked by the one that would kill me, and I didn't even know it.

All the guys went away after a few minutes, and I stayed where we were for more than three hours, trying to understand what had happened to me. I remember that I lay down and stared at the stars of heaven. And I had never seen so much as a shooting star before that night.

LIVING TOGETHER

The experience stayed in my mind for a few days. It was the end of the school year, and classes were coming to end. Two things worried me at this point—not knowing where to buy the "stuff," as the boys called it and that I *unfortunately* had enjoyed it. I had really liked it.

But the clock was ticking; the holidays would begin soon. We were already using about three times a week. The guys who used drugs like this one were almost all the same age as me and my partners. Cocaine was the drug they liked best.

My mother always wondered why I was getting home later, something I had never done before. And I always made some excuse that was not the truth. I would tell her that I was studying or playing ball, since sometimes I came home fast with my emotions high, due to the effect of the cocaine I was snorting with my "friends."

Time passed, and things were getting more serious. We entered the school holiday. This year, I'd still managed to pass my classes even after I'd embraced this miserable, dumb stuff. But it was very hard to do.

When the holidays started, I almost freaked out. I wanted the drug and did not know where to get it. One day, I went back to the same place where we always stayed after school to snort, and I found, to my relief, that the boys were gathering there even without class. *How wonderful*, I thought.

I kept using more and more. I did not know if I was snorting more than three times a week now, but I was for sure doing a much larger quantity than before. The same quantity that I had started using was no longer enough to give me the same effect, the same amazing effect—the dying effect.

With no classes because of vacation, my mother did not understand why I was going to school. I told her we were playing games and championships, and she seemed to accept this answer. I was living with my parents still, but at this time, I spent much of my time out. Sometimes, I went to my parents' house to take a shower and change clothes. But I didn't shower and change often because clean bodies and clothes are not things drug users care much about.

Months passed.

* * *

One day, when I arrived at the place where I always waited for my "friends," they did not come. I waited a little longer, and something happened. My body was shaking. I was a little dizzy and then irritable. I grew even angrier, much more than I would have expected.

One of the colleagues who used the drugs with me showed up to give me the message that there would be no meeting that day. I almost hit him. I was really angry. I could not understand my actions but just acted, or more accurately, reacted.

But he cornered me and told me, "The meeting place has changed. We need to go somewhere else far away. People already know what we're doing here."

We went toward the new spot pretty quickly. I could not stand the waiting. I missed what to me was now a better life. On the way to the new place, I remembered my father's words when I had asked him about the better life. That was the worst advice my father could have given me. He really did not pay attention on this matter, or he didn't care about it.

Perhaps it was fear, perhaps joy—I did not know—but I was thinking about the drugs all the way, and I agonized over it. But what I agonized over more was seeing the cocaine; I was filled with anxiety to get it and obviously to use. Some use drugs to escape from problems, mostly family problems. But my case seemed not to be a problem in my family; the problem was mine. I think the only concern in my family was that my parents did not keep in mind that, during certain phases in young people's lives, it is important to look out for changes and outside influences and steer the child accordingly. I looked at people, and they looked at me suspiciously. It seemed like they knew what I was going to do, it was so funny!

We arrived, finally.

The path we were taking was a dark and dirty way. *How could this be a better life?* I thought. *But what life?*

Oh forget it, I said to myself. *Let's enjoy these moments when I use the powder. Can anyone give me the same euphoria?*

We went through an alley and entered a green, wooden house. Sitting on the porch in a rocking chair was Antonio. When he saw us, he said, "I thought you were not coming. You took too long."

After a pause, he continued. "Paul," he asked, "how will it be now?" I was not even sure if it was a statement or a question, but he looked at me and said, "You have money there."

I was surprised, but I answered, "Not here."

Money? I thought. *For what?*

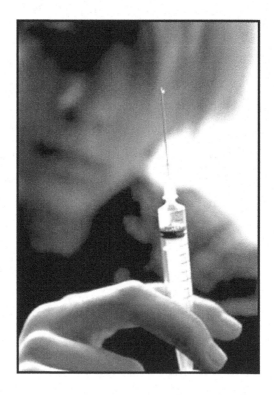

UNCONTROLLED

"Yes, money," said the one who had taken me to that sinister place.

I looked at Antonio without much understanding.

He stared back at me and said coldly, "Hey, man, you think it falls from the sky?"

And I said, "No, I never bothered with that. I have to pay? Is that it?"

And he said, of course; if not, the "firm" breaks.

Okay, I would have to pay; now I knew. And how much was it? I had heard that a small sack of cocaine, about ten grams, cost five to seven dollars. Money was not a great problem for me, but it wasn't available at all times.

Then he asked me to enter the house. He gave me a "little path" that was already ready and said, "Now let's talk."

"Okay," I said.

I waited for him to dispatch a few more people who were calling him from outside the house, and we talked. In fact, that conversation, watered down with a lot of drugs, lasted all night. Suddenly, I realized it was 6:00 a.m. Now what?

An illusion of desire can come from nothing at any time of day and be triggered by any stimulant. Some desires, as I'm sure you all know very well, are like a tapeworm in your gut, sucking out the joy of all. So obviously, some wishes are easier than others to win, subdue, or whatever you do to your wishes. It's like saying you are what your emotions are. You're not sad; you just feel sad. You're not crazy; you're feeling it. It's not you; it's a feeling that you are facing. And you will be happy, you know. Nothing is ever permanent, just like—you guessed it—your desires. You are not what you wish for; you feel a craving.

These were the kinds of thoughts that I began to have; I kept thinking and thinking. Sometimes, I thought I was getting somewhere—calling my attention to something I needed to heed in my own life. Sometimes I thought I was going crazy, freaking out my mind, though I never voiced these thoughts to my friends.

But I had to go home now. I knew I had to face my mother, but that did not bother me much because a mother is a mother. What really worried me was that I'd have to pay to have the stuff in my hands. And today, I was upset with drugs. I was also concerned about how it would be later. That was my real concern. It was my wish, you know!

I went home, went through the backyard, and very slowly entered. My mother was making coffee for breakfast, and this should be the same at any home, no. Your mother gets up early to make coffee.

When I walked in, she immediately asked, "Hey, Paul, where were you at this time?"

It seemed like time stood still, like a type of matrix. I didn't really think much. I just said, "I went to church early, Mother," and I moved to the doorway leading out of the kitchen. It was the only thought that came to me at the moment. I guess my mother either believed me or pretend to.

She became silent.

In Room

I tried hard to sleep, but it seemed I was under severe strain. Some electricity passed through my body and would not let me sleep. It was a mixture of satisfaction and worry about how it would be now, how I would ensure that I could continue to use. I could no longer spend a day without using what in the past had been presented to me as a "happy life.

Despite these thoughts, I fell asleep at last.

* * *

I woke up around noon, and as I said at the beginning of my story, I had lunch and I was wandering through the house and very unhappy. I mean it was not a real unhappiness; sometimes I felt something I didn't even know how to explain. I saw things in black and white all the time. I was like a depressed man. My only concern now was how to pay for my "product."

One year had passed. I was now sixteen years old, and it seems instead of growing, I had decreased in size. I was losing weight. I was not hungry at all. The drugs make you feel like you don't need to eat most of time. The only things that were growing in me were my bones, which were now very visible underneath my skin, turning me into a kind of walking skeleton. But who cared?

I didn't have a girlfriend to try to impress. What concerned me was ensuring that I could use and use more.

The year I turned sixteen, I didn't do well at school. But my family believed this bad performance in school was because of health problems I had. My parents had not caught on to what was going on with me as much as they should have. In the middle of the year, just before I turned sixteen in August, I had a serious lung problem. But everything was resolved, and even then, I didn't stop using. Even after taking the medicine from the doctor, I could not stop. But my parents attributed my thinness to the lung problem, which was very good for me; it was one less problem for me to deal with.

Well, I'd wracked my brain, but I hadn't come up with a solution for how I'd get the money I needed. It actually wasn't much; Antonio told me that for fifty bucks a week, I would have enough drugs to keep me happy. I needed that. The moment was for consumption—the only thing I really cared about was having the drug in hands. And I was sniffing too much. My expenses increased, and I needed money—always.

It was then that I had a wonderful idea. I looked at a beautiful pair of shoes that my mother had given me for a past birthday. *I have to sell them*, I thought. I was no longer using the shoes, but they were still very new. I took them, without guilt, and put them in a bag in my room, and felt a bit more relaxed.

I waited for hours before I went to look for Antonio in his house. Or maybe it wasn't his home. Okay, it doesn't matter now.

As time passed, the evening ended and night came. I took the bag from my room. On my way out, I saw my mom and dad at dinner. They immediately asked if I was sick, because I had not even come out of my room to drink water. And then they immediately asked another question, giving me no time to answer the first. "Where are you going?"

I hadn't thought of a strategy for dealing with the replies to those questions, so I said that I was going to play ball and that was why I was taking the tennis bag. My answer worked well. Maybe it was lack of attention on my parents' part or denial of the problem. Things were not going well for me. Even I knew I was exaggerating. But it seemed like my parents did not see this. The truth is that drug users can manipulate their parents, and most of the time, that worked for me. I cheated them, and they easily believed me.

Well, I got out again, as if I had won another battle, and the lies consumed me fiercely.

I was about to hit rock bottom, and things were about to make a turn for the worse. The shoes were gone, and bad discussions began at home. I started a terrible thing shortly after that night when I took the tennis shoes, but before that, my debts were accumulating more and more.

* * *

To continue to support my drug habit, I started doing something that was even uglier; I began stealing from my parents. For a long time, my parents had wanted to buy a new house, and they kept a few bucks at home. I knew where they kept the money, and starting another stage in my life was quite easy.

When my father realized that money was disappearing, a big fight at home ensued. I had to cry a lot and make myself out to be a victim all the time. I said that I wanted to buy things but was too embarrassed to ask. But my father did not see anything new at home or in my room. He saw that things in my room were always in a mess.

I promised that everything would be fine. I thought, *After all this, what would make a father still believe in a child? Only love, right?* Even though my room was empty and no new goods were showing up, it was hard for my parents to believe that their beloved son was into an awful world like the one I was in.

They tried to believe I was not using drugs, but it was only a matter of time, until they discovered what was going on with me. I thought.

I did not keep my promise again. I began selling stuff—the television, a CD player, my mother's jewelry—all in an attempt to maintain my own addiction. This new behavior was a deep emotional stab in the back for the two people I was supposed to love—one more deception.

Keeping up with this life I had created was getting really hard, and the worst was when I was without the effect of the "better life." The guys who were using with me seemed to be controlled; they dealt with this matter much better than I did. But for me it was different.

DREAMS

If you have faith, your dreams may come true.

The days passed. I completed another year of life. One more August has passed, and my mother prepared a small cake to celebrate and called my old friends.

I had not seen these old friends for a long, long time. They all seemed to not know me anymore. Even when we were talking that day, I was out of my room just to sing happy birthday and then quickly went back. By that time, I was buying—or rather, trading in stolen goods—and taking the drug home. And I did not want to have friends that didn't talk my new language. I was almost certain that all my old friends knew that I was involved with drug. That kind of information runs the streets and turns into gossip, and one of my old friends lived very close to my parents' home.

Inside my room was where my birthday was happening for sure. The cocaine was waiting for me anxiously!

Tonight, I should be celebrating my life, but I was killing my life. I snorted up the cocaine until I passed out.

I did not die that night for God's grace. And speaking of God, I had forgotten him.

The night was horrible. I had horrible dreams with demons chasing me. I ran and ran, but it was no use. They came out of the floor and grabbed at my feet and took me to the great demon, where I had to come face to face with the demon.

I don't know if it was funny or tragic, but I never dreamed of angels. Why?

Well, the experience was truly terrifying. I had to face the "evil" telling me that I was being awaited and that, soon, I would die and go to meet him. I woke up around 5:00 a.m. covered in sweat.

I had nothing to do. Everybody was asleep. A bit of cocaine was left from yesterday that I hadn't been able to sniff. I thought of the dream, that craziness, and I guessed it was the effect of the cocaine. I opened the wardrobe and made another little path for myself. It was my breakfast.

I could not have had an encounter with the bad guy down there, I told myself. My conscience was only telling me that I needed an attitude change. But change what? And why? I was not doing anything bad to anyone.

Another thought suddenly took me. If I could dream about the guy down there, why couldn't I dream of the guy from above? I wanted to dream of God. I really was not a believer. I hadn't been in church for a long time, but I had learned about God from my mother.

As much as I used the drug, I sometimes felt empty. I had grown up hearing that God fulfilled us with peace and rebirth. But it was not happening to me yet.

Had God abandoned me? Or not?

Long ago, I'd read that dreams were a kind of manifestation of desires. Perhaps, then, I was worried about the devil or I wanted to talk to him. Maybe I was trying to decide what path I wanted my life to follow. As I said, I had a dream about the devil when I almost passed away in my room at my birthday party.

Ah, but those concerns were quickly falling behind, replaced by new concerns. How would I get money to buy more? In fact, it was already two o'clock. I realized that I was a guy who thought too much, who reflected too often. Even when I was using, I was always thinking about what was going on around me or what had happened.

But now, how would I manage to consume?

CRUDE REALITY

I thought maybe I could ask Antonio or Marcos, another acquaintance I'd made during the two years of my cocaine habit, if I could borrow some cocaine and pay later. Would they believe that I would pay later? I had been with them for a long time, and this could be good for me. Anyway, I was their friend, and one cannot leave a friend behind, I told myself

I pulled myself up with courage and went to meet up with Antonio. He was the guy who had first presented this poor, cruel life to me, but I liked him.

I arrived in the alley, and there was the guy at the same location, with the same face of evil, awaiting buyers or the living dead who were in search of a little more of poison in order to calm their fears and feed the animals inside their bodies.

I came and talked to him, and to my chagrin, he said that he needed to make money with the drugs he had and could not give them away for free to anybody. He said that he knew I could make money somehow. He hardly knew that I had nothing. In that moment, I thought that I had to keep stealing from my family.

Man, this time I felt like crap. I felt despicable, and I despised myself. But, my friend, this parallel world is like that! Drugs make you dishonest. When the money flows away, we must take from anywhere we can.

What to do, where to go, I thought. Or rather, in my thoughts, I swept my house. I thought of every object there—DVDs, cell phone, wallets, earrings, the freezer, the refrigerator, the stove. These were absurd thoughts, but it was the way, the weird way I had to walk. I had to get something.

And then I remembered Marcos, another friend who could help me. Or maybe not.

I got home in a hurry. And you know, I was not tired. I had run nearly fifteen miles and arrived feeling well. I was an athlete . . . or a wild, hungry animal! Choose.

It was eight o'clock at night. My family was awake watching TV. I went into the house, and for the first time, my parents looked at me face to face. I looked at them. I felt as if I was under an X-ray machine, and I saw how they saw me—a walking skeleton, with torn pants and underwear appearing above my low pants, dirty teeth, and hard and messy hair. They became frightened.

"My son?" said my mother, sure that I was not in a normal state. "What happened? You're so thin, so anemic. Are you sick?"

It's amazing that some parents take too many years to see what is happening inside their own house. And it is a crude fact that these parents take too long to perceive that one of their sons or daughters is using this poison.

I said I was okay.

But at this moment, my father spoke, and for the first time, he screamed. "Hey there. Sit here," he demanded. And he asked to talk to me. He preached to me about my behavior. He asked about the friendships that I had overlooked and the new friends he had never met. He asked about the school I had left. This was the second year that I had not gone to school. And my father, for the first time, told me something.

My mom and dad had realized I was out of school for a while, but they'd poured time away believing I would attend again, just waiting for this phase to pass, to end.

And what could I say? I listened to everything my parents said very quietly. Between their speeches, I said often that it was okay, that they shouldn't worry.

Then my mom asked a question that was the last thing I wanted to hear, "Are you using drugs?"

Ouch, the question was for me like a sword through my heart. Even though I was using drugs, hearing this from the mother's mouth was very annoying and took away all my desire to live!

The matrix had happened again in my life. Suddenly, a flash affected my mind. I thought I saw several moments of my life appearing before me—the moment of beginning; the moment of recklessness; the time of agony, of theft, of trade; my serious intentions of being able to stop using; the moments that I thought, alone, on the paths I took; the moments that I was a self-styled great thinker. Hey, I saw everything.

And then the matrix was over, and it was time for me to answer the question, "Are you using drugs?" It was time to say yes or no.

Saying yes would be complete incompetence; I would confess that I was doing a completely wrong thing in their view, and I knew how they would think about it. If I said no, I'd deny the truth and lie to the people I loved most. So what was I to do?

It was then that I took the attitude of shouting and retorting. I could not believe what I was coming out of my mouth. I accused them of slander. I shouted profanities; I said slangs that I never spoken at home.

I shouted so loud that my parents were brought to apologize for what they had asked me. But deep inside, I knew that, from this time on, things would change. Their eyes would be more clinical, and I needed to prepare myself to get better and better at pretending for Mom and Dad.

When they put me against the wall, pushing me to say the truth about my poor life, I had to take an evasive action. I did not have anything to say.

I left the house slamming the door fiercely and spent my first two days away from home.

And that was just the first of several fights inside my home now that my parents suspected that I was using drugs. I even pulled a knife on my mother and pushed my father hard, causing him to fall and break his leg.

Mommies always try to believe that their children aren't doing wrong things. And that a family member may be abusing drugs is the last option any family wants to consider. I knew that.

On the day I pulled the knife, I was very stressed by the need to use. I asked my mom for money, and she did not give it to me, saying she didn't have it. And it was the truth. But I did not believe her and thought that she was against me or didn't love me enough. And you know, I wanted to kill her. As horrible as it is, I wanted to kill her. In the midst of our discussion I lost my mind and grabbed a knife. My father saw it all and ran at me, but I pushed him with so much force that he fell and broke his leg.

I am filled with regret and sadness today when I remember that day. Today I am twenty-one years old, going on twenty-two. I'm fine, but my story is not over yet.

All the Same

Time passed. I was almost eighteen years old. I had used cocaine for a long time.

I started experimenting with free-base cocaine basis, a modality of the drug that is smoked. But I did not like it because it left my fingers all yellow and dark. The police had already caught me once. They already knew who used this dreg of drug. I used to put my fingers in bleach, trying to clean them. But the bleach no longer took over the stain, and I needed to rub my fingers on the asphalt. That hurt a lot.

After Antonio denied me, refusing to give me the drug and let me pay later, I abandoned him. It had been about six months since I had seen him. I'd begun a closer relationship with Marcos, and he was the one who had supported me when I first fought with my parents.

Marcos was my partner now. I was almost living in his house, and there we had other experiences, some of them very weird effects of the drugs. We used together and sold together.

Marcos lived much better than Antonio. His house was very well furnished, but I did not understand a thing. I was losing everything because of drugs, and Marcos had everything. It seemed that for him, the drug did not cause the same damage that it caused me. What was the difference?

At this point, I started to sell drugs to sustain my vice. Marcos and I were now drug dealers. This was worse than using.

One day, he came to me and said, "Will we know something amazing today?"

Man, I froze. It seemed that a gift would fall into my hands. But what would be even better than cocaine?

He said it was "the rock," more commonly known as crack, and it was different dreg. It did not dirty the hands and fingers if you knew how to use the right tools.

That was when we began a journey, a journey with crack—violent but good. Crack goes to your brain rapidly and makes you very high, much higher than does cocaine, despite that it is made of cocaine. But addiction goes faster as well. With the first puff into the lungs the "matrix," mixed with a "Superman" feeling came. This feeling was like I could accomplish anything, like an energy fuel surged inside of me. I was flying very slowly, and after the effect wore off, I fell quickly and fiercely. It would even hurt at given moments. But all in all, crack was a unique experience.

At home, things were black. My mother called the priest to talk to me. I fooled him, saying that I would return to church, but in the end, nothing!

I talked to many psychologists, and nothing worked. It seemed I knew more than them; I fooled them all. In front of them, I accepted all they said, but once they'd turned their backs, I was doing the opposite.

I was still using crack during the nights and staying overnight at Marcos's place.

But I needed to help Marcos. He told me that, even though he had more money than I did, he would not pay for our addiction alone. Marcos's father was a big city attorney, even very rich, but I had to work. I had to pay, and at my home, things went very badly. I had nothing to steal from there; I could take hardly anything of value.

I started to commit small assaults. I robbed people and spent much of my day in the markets looking for opportunities where I was sure not to lose. I always got back to Marcos's home with some money in my pocket, so my life would continue—and so my death would keep coming. I did not notice that!

My very first robbery was at a market. I saw an old woman buying her needs, and I waited for her to finish. When she went to her car, I followed her. And just when she turned the corner of the parking garage, I pushed her fiercely and took almost all her belongs. I took her purse, her rings, and her wallet. The poor lady screamed loudly, but no one came.

You cannot imagine what a junkie will do in order to get the drug he "needs."

Marcos's father took a big case out of town and needed to move away. Marcos and his father lived alone. His mother had been dead for ten years. One day, Marcos's dad called him and said they would move to the other city. The idea that Marcos would be relocating got me down. I felt really sad.

Marcos readily accepted the move. In fact, I was just another junkie; I was not a friend. I was a junkie for use only; ours was not a sincere friendship. The parties we had, the girls we got—it was only a theater of life, and not reality. No way.

Once again, I felt alone, and for the first time, I thought about my parents, you know, like the prodigal son. Even far away from the Bible, I remembered this story. Madness, is not it?

Marcos was gone, and no sign that he would return was forthcoming.

I felt some fatigue, but I did not care much. I returned home, apologized, and lied, saying I wanted to get treatment and that I could no longer stand this life. But I only said it so that I could be home again, in peace.

My parents welcomed me back. That night was horrible, really, really bad. I wanted to use but had to strive to not give in.

Only those who have been through addiction know what I am talking about. Drugs, as a matter of fact, control you and make you seems like a puppet.

In the dark of the night, I remembered Antonio.

Again Antonio

My absence from the drug was now more ferocious. The crack leaves a hole deep inside you—an emptiness, a kind of absence of mind or soul or something. It was really heavy.

But Antonio would have what I needed to fill that emptiness—at least momentarily.

I saw in my closet my tennis shoes, which I'd somehow forgotten about. I would take the shoes and pay a visit to Antonio, my old friend, the next morning.

See, one becomes an unscrupulous person, full of lies; it is amazing.

I went in search of Antonio. To my surprise, he loved the shoes, and we renewed our friendship!

He wanted me to participate in sales now. Antonio said that we would use less and sell more. We had to make money that way. He said we would sell to the boys we knew from school. The school—it had already been so long since I'd thought about my old school.

Antonio also had crack to sell. And with the shoes, I could get some stones for myself. But I was worried about two things—how to get more things to exchange for crack and the promise I had made at home that I would stop using drugs and seek treatment. Such a promise is not an easy thing to carry out.

I was really worried.

I told myself I was a different kind of drug user; I thought a lot. Yeah, there I was thinking again.

Then suddenly, it occurred to me that once I started selling with Antonio, I would have money. But what could I do about my family?

This was matter for concern later. For now, I would enjoy what would come.

The situation with Antonio went very well. We were selling a lot. But my desire was to consume drugs, not sell them. I used all of the money I made from sales for my own use, and nothing was left for myself.

Occasionally I visited my family. They seemed tired of me, willing to get rid of me—not me but my despicable behavior and my comings and goings.

I stayed away from home for weeks. My health was precarious. I used to feel severe pain in my back. I once read that crack killed soon, but I lasted a long time. I had been using crack for two years already. I was nearing twenty and was already an adult, but I had no thoughts about stopping and no desire to do so. I still thought the drugs were good to me. I was a thinker. I thought a lot and hoped it would help me in the future. But they were just thoughts and no action.

One time when I was visiting my mother, she asked me to speak to the priest at the church near my house. It seemed like a smart idea at the time, perhaps because I was kind of thoughtful at the moment. Well, I was not normal, but I just went to talk to the priest.

But nothing worked. He wanted me to be hospitalized, and I, of course, refused.

I believed deep in my heart that I would stop when the right moment come. All users are accustomed to saying that. We pretend to know we can control this—can control our vices.

I was at the height of enjoyment. I was terrible, but I felt good. Treatment now—why?

A little more time passed. I was still on crack, and sometimes, for lack of crack, I snorted cocaine again. But cocaine did not satisfy me anymore. After the episode with the priest, I returned to sleep at home again. But the atmosphere was terrible. My father seemed to hate me; he had ever since I pushed him. He was fine, but the hurt was still there. Sometimes I heard Dad say to Mom that he would hand me over to the police even though sending a son to jail was not right. But I wasn't worried that my father would take any action.

I kept working with Antonio.

DEATH EXCHANGE

I went to Antonio's and found him snorting a little path.

Shortly after I arrived, we heard someone shouting Antonio's name from out in front of the hut. Antonio went to see who it was.

In a flash, I heard a gunshot and soon after three more shots. I did not know what to do. I hid under a table in Antonio's old kitchen. I remained there frozen for a few minutes, and then I heard footsteps entering the house and ferocious screaming.

"Where are these junkies?" roared a man's voice. "I'll kill everyone. I have to break up this den of wickedness that exists here. One has already been sent to hell. Where are the others?"

I was petrified. I did not know what to do. And the "matrix" took hold of me again. Time stopped, and I started thinking about my family and myself. It was a kind of farewell because I thought I would die right there.

The steps came closer and closer. The man searched the room, overturning everything. Suddenly, he pulled the tablecloth up and saw me there.

But something happened. I don't know how it happened, but I had my hands together as if in prayer. He looked at me and said, pointing a gun at me, "Pray and change your life, you bastard. I'll spare you because I saw you praying." He turned around.

Before going, he came back to give me a kick, but he did not shoot.

I didn't know what to say. Only one phrase echoed in my mind—*thank God*. I remembered God now.

But the worst—or at least the worst scene to be seen by my eyes—was coming. After a few minutes of remaining frozen, I got up and went outside to see what had happened with Antonio.

Suddenly, Mommy's thought came to my mind; *God's showing His greatness in what the world saw as a tragedy*. Wow, Mommy really was a great believer.

I went outside and saw a lot people stealing the bags of drugs that were in Antonio's pocket. No one bothered to help him. I realized that what Antonio had gathered around himself was a crowd of dumb animals in need of a disastrous food—the drugs.

I looked at Antonio, who had no face. One of the shots had hit him in the head and destroyed his face. Antonio was no longer Antonio. He was a lot of discarded meat. And people were moving in, vultures picking through the carrion. What a hellish sight.

I took in the infernal sight. What would I do now? I thought back to my family, and I decided to go home.

Going home, I thought a lot. The image of Antonio stayed in my mind, and his bloody body was disastrous image. But what impressed me most were the people—the vultures eating their carrion. And I was one of them. The difference was that I was not eating carrion that time, perhaps because I had suffered a worse scare than they had—having a gun to my head.

I was thinking too much.

I saw my parents again and took a shower. I wanted to wash that dust away from me.

I do not know what time I got home, but I know I walked almost the whole morning, and without using drugs. For the first time in four years, I spent a night without drugs. I went home.

AT HOME

At home, I could not sleep; I could not even close my eyes. I was weak, and I needed to rest. My mother asked surprised and she did not understand all that was going with me.

A silence came over me. I heard a voice. I did not know if I was going crazy or if the voice was real. It was not my mother's voice. The voice said, "Come on. Make your choice. It's time. You need to choose."

You know, it seemed like I was getting a chance or something. I thought about how the guy had found me under the table.

Let me tell you a little about the situation of the shooter, and then I'll come back to my mental ramblings. The man who left me under the table was the father of one of the thousands of users, or vultures who were there all day. I even knew the guy, but I was not a friend of his. His name, if I'm not mistaken, was Savio. Savio's father had suffered lot and had seen his son suffer. Savio had pulmonary emphysema and was very ill in the hospital—indeed, he was between life and death, a place that was not life, a place where even death would almost be better. Drugs kill.

That night, the boy had left this life for a better one, as they say. The father was totally upset and went after his son's slow killer, Antonio, who was actually on drugs. This is the short story. It took that man, Savio's father, to kill Antonio and make me reflective as well.

At home, I was very weak. I needed a mother's lap. The mother's lap replenishes our energy. Those of you who have not found comfort in the laps of your mothers should drop everything and go running to your mother and feel how healing her warmth and love is.

I did not know what to think. I was stunned. I was confused. I felt a desire to snort drugs again. But I was overwhelmed by fear, and the image of the gun against my head and the man's voice telling me to go and change my life had crystallized in my mind.

I decided that I would change. But my mind changed just as quickly.

I'd heard that staying away from the drug was almost impossible. Was it true? If so, I was doomed to die. I was reluctant to believe that after the experience I had just lived through, so I slept.

And I finally dreamed the dream that had thus far eluded me.

GOD

I had once dreamed about "the guy down there." I occasionally wondered why I had never dreamed of God, even after the episode with the gun in my face. I thought God was no longer interested in me. But tonight was different. I dreamed about Jesus, and He said nothing but walked by my side for a beautiful way. This gave me much pleasure and satisfaction. I walked barefoot, and we seemed to understand one another. I was in Him, and He was in me—it was transcendental, something I had never even lived with the "aid of drugs." I lived that unforgettable dream often in my life.

And I kept dreaming.

I did not speak, and neither did Jesus. But I fully understood. I realized that I received his directions all the time and that he was at my side at all times. He made me see all the times that He had been on my side and I had not perceived his presence because of the influence of drugs. I was completely ecstatic and blissful.

From drugs to Jesus, there I was. When our spiritual conversation had come to an end, He pulled a twig from the forest floor and asked me, now in an audible voice, "Son, do you want to change?"

And I said, "Yes, my Lord."

He then said that my case would be solved only if that was what I wanted and made a knot in the twig He had pulled. I did not quite understand, but I accepted.

And suddenly, I woke up.

Now Jesus was gone. It was four in the morning. For a few moments, I had lived out of my body and had not felt the influence of the body in my decisions, but now back here, I would come to feel this influence.

And at the moment of awakening, I missed the damn drug, crack.

*   *   *

I hesitated again and found some of my "friends," who were also friends of the now deceased Antonio. Together, we went in search of new suppliers. I relaxed a bit, because I had a certain amount of crack to sell, the amount that Antonio had given me before he died.

But I did not sell the crack. I used it, and whenever the effects of the drugs were gone, I remembered Jesus and my mother. I was about to turn twenty-one years old and had lost five years of my life in this whirlwind of madness that seemed to never stop.

My God, I did not find another crack provider. I only found a source of cocaine, and I had to go back to the one that had embraced me first. It was like a destiny that seemed to chase me. Once more, I had no strength to resist drugs. Even after I had dreamed of Jesus, I couldn't muster the force to do it. And I fell again.

My mother suffered a lot. My father had not talked to me in years. I had had several opportunities to change. I did not. Hey, how many people dreams about Jesus and have the experience I had? I think few.

I was a wreck, but I maintained an outward appearance of health. One day, a strange thing happened. I was in the middle of the street when I felt a violent pain in right in the middle of my chest. I had just sniffed a lot of cocaine in the spot where I was now taking the drug. I simply fell to the ground and fainted. This time, I did not see Jesus; what a pity.

I don't know who led me to the emergency room. After a few hours, I woke up and saw my mother sitting on the floor because Brazil's emergency rooms offer very little comfort. I saw that scene—one more disappointment involving me. *I am nothing*, I thought.

I thought that I had come into this world just to make those who love me suffer.

At once, I called my mother and said, "Mother, I will change." "Son," she told me, "do not promise me anything."

At that time, I did not understand my mother. But today I understand. She could no longer support false promises, and God knows how much I had promised and promised.

But it seemed different to me, and that was when I said, "Mom, I want help." Well that I had never told her. And then I saw a brief small smile on her face, and I thought it would be the best thing to do.

She stood up and said, "God bless you."

I never felt so much peace. Even here, in an emergency room stretcher, I felt a great peace, much like the peace I felt in the hand of Jesus.

I thought, *I will begin a new phase in my life*. And I was really willing to do it—to change and get treatment.

But then the doctor came to the clinic and told me in a deep, angry voice—it seemed that he was angry with the world, or perhaps he did not like drug users, "Look, you're gonna die the next time."

I remembered the guy down there, who had said he would be waiting for me when I died. Would I go to Jesus or the devil? I had to choose.

Choosing wasn't an easy thing to do. My new drug habits involved me in situations that had previously been unknown to me.

Now that I looked back on the first time I'd tried the drugs, it seemed that resisting could have been so easy. Then I would have never met the evil that I was now so wrapped up in. But that was not the case.

Then I said, "Oh my God." Starting to use drugs had been so easy. Leaving it was difficult.

CHANGE

Under the watchful eye of my mother and my father, the doctor also made several other recommendations, specifying that drugs could kill me and cause various functions of the body to malfunction. Though my father was there physically, he seemed emotionally distant from me. I wondered if he was only there at the insistence of my mother or if he was really worried about me.

But at that time, it did not matter. What mattered was that he was there with me. The doctor once again related experiences with other drug users and said that the end was always tragic. He recommended a clinical hospital to my mother. And thus began another phase in my life.

I didn't imagine how difficult this phase would be, but I was willing to fight, at least at that moment there.

When we got back home, my mother gave me all the care and love she had to give. I was like a baby. But then, after a brief interval of time, I began to feel a desire, a kind of a longing. I wanted to use and use fast. A kind of anger, or rather, a strange irritation began to take hold of me.

I began to respond to anything my mother said—my father remained silent—with brutal words. An incredible change had come over me between the time I was at the emergency room and now back at my house. My mother suffered greatly in this process, and now I see that my father did too. But he was usually more distant. Typically it's the mother who has to deal with the difficulties of a child's drug abuse, and she suffers immensely.

Mom called to the clinic the doctor had suggested and made an appointment for me for the next day. I was upset with the rush, but deep down, I knew it could not wait too long, as I could give up.

I went the next day. That last night at home was a horror. My mother, frightened, slept in my room. She was afraid that I'd go out at night and not come back. She watched me all night long. It was a very bad night, not because my mother stayed with me, but I was craving for the drug.

I did not sleep well. I could never have imagined that a person could be like that without drugs or that a simple substance could leave a human being like that. That's when I remembered the "vultures" over the "carrion" when Antonio was killed. The drug makes men and women turn into animals.

When I arrived at the clinic, a professional was waiting to talk with me. First, he spoke with my mother while I waited. And then he called me and interviewed me. I answered the questions he asked me, but unfortunately, I did not tell him everything. I hardly say anything to a person I do not know. I thought a big part of my life wasn't anyone else's business. Why would I tell him everything?

Too many things—my deep emotions, my huge hollow inside, my fears, my lack of determination—remained unsaid.

He said we could start treatment soon, and I'd be there for at least six months. This made a pretty big impact on me, but the biggest shock was learning that my mother would not be able to see me until I had completed the first ninety days. I had to begin the treatment immediately, but one thing was bursting inside of me. I wouldn't see my mommy again for ninety days from that moment. It was important as, according to the clinic, seeing one's loved ones too soon could affect the cure.

It was tragic, but the interviewer asked, "Weren't you on the street day after day, without thinking of your mother?"

Yeah, this was true. But who was he to tell me that? I didn't even know him.

Friends, treatment began. The participants shared many spiritual moments and developed a strong fellowship with one another. The clinic was where we shared our difficulties with others, which was very good. But the solitude was great too. I saw people inside going nuts due to the loneliness. The time I liked best was the nights, when I could talk openly with the monitors. They were mostly ex-addicts who knew what we suffered, and we could talk frankly.

But Jacob soon appeared, and this guy was crazy. Let me tell you about Jacob's first day.

I had been there for about fifteen days, and Jacob arrived and brought with him several packages of cannabis resin. He said it was to give him relief during the nights. He offered it to everyone and asked us not to tell the monitors. He also said that the stuff was to relieve the loneliness.

For three long days, I was reluctant to accept Jacob's proposal. But on the fourth day, I took him up on his offer. I had been inside for almost twenty days, and I was very sad and lonely.

Thus began another phase of my using, this one inside a clinical, amazingly.

Let me tell you, and I will not hide anything.

Clinic I

I was already using marijuana or, as they called it inside, the "little black cigar." But no one knew, or at least they pretended they didn't. Deep inside, I knew that the monitors knew all that happened there, but they let the marijuana use go because they also knew it was difficult to endure as much pain inside.

A month passed, but it felt like a year. And ninety days were like an eternity. I wanted to see my mother. I asked all the time to make a call so that I could talk to my parents. But the monitors always said it would disrupt the treatment. All right, all right noted. But what to do? I had to withstand all of that if I wanted to clean myself up and eliminate the drugs from my life.

And what do you think I'd do?

The suffering days were passing, and the sun rose and sank each day. As I said before, I was using marijuana inside, but I wanted more. I wanted something stronger. I was very irritable when I was asking Jacob for other "stuff." I meant cocaine.

He sternly said, "Hey, man, I'm not a charity man. You want this, you pay for this. You have to pay for what you want."

I was again in shock, not because Jacob was charging—everyone charged—but because drugs were being sold in a place that was supposed to treat addicts. What had we come to? Neither the monitors nor the CEO seemed to know what was going on there.

Here in the clinic, the drug trade continued, and the parents out there thought the recovering addicts were safe. Look, I can't say that all clinics have the same thing going on, but this was the case in the clinic I was in.

Then I stepped back and thought again, as usual. I was a thinker. And my thoughts were about my life and the commitments I had made to go through my treatment. But I could not stand by this commitment much longer. And I had already premeditated my escape. The clinic was more than 40 kilometers from my home, along a road that connected one city to another.

I waited until evening, and then I jumped the wall, which was not high, and started walking. This was no problem for a person who had walked for hours and even days in the middle of all kinds of people. Walking on a road could be even better, I thought.

I had tried to achieve my goal. I had already done thirty-nine days in the clinic. But I couldn't stand it. My journey on foot was consumed more by thoughts of what I was going to say to my mother than the fatigue itself, so much so that I was not tired.

I thought about my childhood before I'd turned fifteen; those were wonderful moments. And now, here I was fleeing from a house for junkies. What a big change.

It was dawn, and I was still far from arriving at my house. There came a cruel urge. Since I was here and my mother did not know where I was, perhaps before I went home, I could just pass by to see and talk to some "friends" and see if they could fix me up something to use. It was a cruel temptation, no? What would you do, dear reader?

I won; I went home. But I would have been better if I had gone to get drugs because, when I got home, we fought on all sides. My mother cried out in anger. My father spoke again. "Boy," he said, "do you know how much I paid for you to stay inside? I paid five thousand dollars. I had to borrow money, and you simply run away!

That's when they paused, and I said, "There was a guy in there selling drugs. I asked to call you, but they wouldn't allow me to. I was homesick, and I was using drugs inside. I would have freaked out if I'd continued inside."

In truth, it was not because of the drugs that I wanted to escape. It was because I did not want to stay right there. But the excuse "stuck." My father calmed down and immediately called the clinic asking for his money back, or at least part of the money.

The trouble got bigger. The clinic did not return the money because they said I had given up and quit. The contract we'd signed stated no compensation would be paid in cases where the patient quit.

After that, my dad was filled with a mix of anger toward me, which was not good, and an even stronger hatred of the clinic that would not return the money he'd invested.

It was not long before my mother was looking for a pastor friend so I could go to another clinic; she didn't want me to stay at home.

Addicts' families can become so worn out that, often, they just want to see the drug user far away. Today, I do not blame them; taking care of a drug user is very difficult. But in those days, I was angry, just thinking they did not want me around.

Mom took two days to find another clinic. I was distressed. During those two days, my father tied me by the feet to the fridge. It was absurd. He did it to keep me from fleeing home. Those were bad days, making me miss the first clinic and feel sorry that I'd fled.

I sat there, tied up, with a mad urge to use drugs, even agonizing. I eventually try to cut my wrists with a knife with so much anguish but did not reach the drawer of knives from my mother.

After the two days of being tied up was over, I was taken to another clinic. It was ugly-looking. Imagine, a ramshackle house with fifteen young people inside. The first thing I saw when I entered was a boy who had been wounded in the head with a knife during a street fight. Another resident had a prison tattoo, and so on. I quietly thought, *I'll die here; this will be my death.*

Clinic II

Mom bet everything with this new opportunity, as she said. I stayed. Here I would be allowed visits during the first month. I would not have to wait ninety days to see my mother. My father did not want to know anything about me; he would stay at home again, like the first time. The warrior was my mother.

And so began a new stage in my life, inside another clinic. Now I felt loneliness, but this loneliness was not as strong as it was when I was in the first clinic. I was even more afraid of being with those guys there than of being away from my parents. Various sorts of people were inside, and most of them were very young like me.

I thought at once about how the drugs had reached all spaces of our society and destroyed too many families in the world. Who would help us?

Were we lost?

The days passed in much the same way they had in the other clinic. But in this second clinic, there was no professional who was responsible for us. It was us taking care of ourselves. Everything—the care, the guidance, the steps of AA, and everything else—was handled by ex-drug users. And this was something that nobody respected, because what kind of moral obligation would one drug user have to another?

The owner of the clinic turned his back, and the residents started the mess. I believed that clinics like that must have professionals like psychologists, therapists, social workers and so on. What I could not understand was ex-junkies taking care of others. Dealing with and leading these kinds of people—I mean people who are involved with drugs—is not an easy task.

More than three months passed, and I felt like I'd been there for a long time. The treatment at this second clinic lasted for four months. I had completed 80 percent of the treatment. My father had never been on a visit, but my mother never missed one.

It was then that the owner of the clinic called me to talk to me and proposed that I become a monitor. Me, a monitor? What could I teach to the guys?

But I accepted the challenge. I wanted to give my mom something that she could be proud after so much trouble and work.

The clinic owner told me about the work of the monitors and introduced me as a monitor to the rest of the guys, which was cause for much laughing. So it was with all the monitors; this is how they were all treated.

And then I thought, *Things with me will be different. These guys will have to respect me.* After all, I was the monitor, the responsible one.

The first to arrive and give me a warning was the guy who had been wounded in the head with a knife. He warned me not to mess with him. He looked me straight in the eyes and said, "I'm on my own. Do not touch me, ever."

I wondered how I would be a good monitor. I was screwed!

For a long time, I hadn't read the Bible. I mean, I was not a good reader at all. But I remembered the perusal of my mother. She used to read snippets to m sometimes. But that day I was so scared that I opened the Holy Word, as my mother called and read Psalm 23, which says, "The Lord is my Shepherd. I shall not want."

I stopped and stared at that sentence for long minutes, trying to memorize what that psalm meant to me at that moment. Sleepiness came. I went to sleep. The fear still gripped me, but I was more comforted by the words of the Bible.

And reading the Bible must be a daily practice for us. If you still don't do this, start! You will be fine and happier!

Some words of the Bible give hope and make us see what is veiled. Inside of the clinic, we noticed how we need God's presence. And sometimes fear gripped me because of what had happen to me. When I was cleaned of drugs, I saw I could go onward.

MONITOR

On my first day as a monitor, I took the daily book and called everyone to order the breakfast. The kitchen staff had already prepared our meal, and I needed to join everyone at the table to eat, but I needed to pray first. I read the same passage of the Psalms and prayed for all. My prayer was quick but with a lot of willingness deep inside. I even let tears roll down my face, and I saw that the tattooed guy cried out as well. I thought, *Hey, I have a friend.*

The only one who didn't come to the table was the guy who'd been wounded in the head with a knife. The owner asked me to go call him in the room and say that, if he did not come now, would miss the breakfast.

I did what he asked, but the fear was great. I called to him at the room.

He cried, "My head is about to explode with pain. Help me."

I did not know what to do. I entered the room and saw him lying on the ground. I ran and called the owner of the clinic. He came quietly, saw the boy on the floor, and said, "This is nothing. It is only 'bad spirit.' Pray and it will go away.

But I saw something else. Okay, it could be a "bad spirit," but the pain was real, and he needed help. I told the owner that he should take the boy to the emergency room.

"Junkie boys have to suffer," he replied.

Those words were like knives in my breast. Okay, so he thought that junkie boys had to suffer, but we were paying him so that we could receive treatment. He called this place a clinic, and he could not do that.

Now, I did not know what to do. If I got out of there, my mother would be hurt again. Until I explained that red is not black, to give up would be awful. So I thought fast and was comforting the young man, who had so much fear. The only thing I could think of to do was to pray. I sat beside him; put his head, which was very hot, in my lap; and began to pray. I wasn't sure what I was saying, but I was praying fervently.

I stayed until he fell asleep. When I left the room, I got an earful from the owner. "Look, I did not make you monitor for you to be treating these guys well," he told me.

I passed by him and wondered what had happened. But I was feeling good about what I had done for the guy. And I thought another phase of my life was beginning.

I turned my attention to other tasks, including checking that everything was in line for lunch. But a thought wouldn't leave my mind. Did I have some healing power? When I'd prayed, the injured boy had slept. Was it for this that God had given me life? And for the first time in my life, I was answering the question I had asked myself in the emergency bed, when I had seen my mother sitting on the floor after I got sick in the street. Did God have a purpose for my life?

Have you ever asked yourself about that—about whether your life is a project of God's?

* * *

The days passed. The boy with the headache did not feel anything after the episode in his room. I had already been inside for six months of treatment, three months of which I was a monitor. But I didn't intend to stay there for the rest of my days.

I started thinking about asking to leave because I felt good. I was really cool and wanted to live out there in the real world again, to prove to myself that the treatment was good, to prove to my mother that I was good and healed and could be believed again, and so that my father could call me son again. These days in the clinic had made me grow up. I thought more clearly about my life and family. Sure it was not enough to keep me from eventually going back to drugs, but in each new treatment, we can learn more and know that life is priceless.

But how I would do this was another matter. I was concerned because, when my mother had last come to visit, she'd told me to stay there longer. She'd said, "Son, do not rush to leave. Everything is fine out there. Your father is well. We are hoping that everything will be all right with you too."

And the more I said I was well, the more she asked me to stay a bit more.

As for the owner of the clinic, he said, "It is better if you stay a little longer."

And how much longer would that be, twenty years?

Shutdown

I did not want to spend the rest of my life stuck in that clinic. I began to worry about how I would make my way out.

I already believed that I no longer needed any more treatment. In fact, I was no longer in treatment. I was treating others, which I didn't want to do but had to accept in order to get along with the owner of the clinic.

I wanted freedom. I thought I had already suffered too much. I wanted to be free of drugs.

I planned my conversation with Mr. Peter for days. He was the one I had to talk to. After more than a month of continuing to suffer, I finally talked to him. The conversation took place soon after the family visit on the last Sunday of the month. My mother, by the way, had left again feeling good, as Mr. Peter had praised me a lot to her.

I waited for nightfall and asked to speak with him before he went to sleep. I told him I wanted to get out. I had been there for seven months and believed it would be okay to leave. I asked his opinion about my condition.

He became angry and said he thought I was not ready and that I'd fall back into drugs. He said I was being stupid, but he could not stop me. Then he gave me an injection of discouragement. He said I was going to fall again and again into the gutter, and I did not want that to happen.

This conversation made me stay fifteen more days, bearing the place where I no longer wanted to live.

It was the most harrowing fifteen days I remember. I was trying not to think about leaving, but the anxiety hit me when night came. And it came back; the desire to leave was a desire like the desire to use drugs. I wanted freedom, and I watched the days passing. I no longer wanted to be a monitor and be responsible for the boys.

My discontent was apparently obvious. John, the boy who had been wounded, wanted to know what was going on with me. I no longer spoke. I just wanted to know how I was going to get out.

When I'd completed the fifteen tedious days and could no longer bear being there, I went to talk again with Mr. Peter. "Mr. Peter, I'm leaving," I said. Those were the most courageous words of my life.

I went to get my things, and he followed me into the room. In a threatening tone, he said, "You'll fall, and I will not want you here anymore."

But now my leaving was for real.

When he saw I was determined, Mr. Peter called me and said, "I want you to attend a clinic outside that belongs to a friend of mine." He gave me the address. It was an outpatient treatment clinic. Patients received treatment during the day and went home every day or every few days.

I took the old piece of paper with the address on it and went out to meet the street again. I said good-bye to everyone, and now without fear, I went looking for my freedom. I didn't know what was going on out there or how I would be received at home. But I was happy, and that was more important.

I went out and took the road. I would not ask the clinic to call my mother this time. I wanted to give her a good surprise. I walked and then hitched a ride with a trucker who was passing by. I arrived at my home and tried to peacefully explain everything and how it was all good. I told my parents that I felt safe and, particularly, that Mr. Peter had given me the address of an outpatient clinic. I explained that it was a clinic that did not require the recovering drug user to be a resident.

Mom and Dad did not believe that the clinic would work. That was when I made a promise. I would go to the clinic and attend treatment regularly or I would leave the house.

But I wanted my father's forgiveness. Without that, I could not live.

My father looked at me with stern eyes and was silent for a moment.

FORGIVENESS

The moment I had thought of so many times—imagining how it would be—finally came. The two most impactful moments of my life—when I was sitting under Antonio's table facing a man who was holding a gun to my head and when I was holding the head of an injured boy in my lap facing the uncaring clinic owner—had one thing in common. During these two moments, I had relied on a strategy that I never used at any other time in my life—prayer. Would it all be worth it now?

But I was very nervous about the piercing gaze of my father. He had remained silent since the day I pushed him down and pulled a knife on my mother, as if to punish me. I did not say anything else; they both also stopped talking. I went to my room, thinking of praying. But I was so nervous I could not pray at all.

That was when a very strong feeling came over me, a craving for using drugs. It seemed to erupt from within me. Someone had once told me that crack was overwhelming, and I had not believed. It seemed that my moment had arrived. I writhed around. I was extremely dizzy and had severe pain in my neck and back. I had cramps and was filled with anger.

I didn't know what to do. What came to my mind was that I should go out and buy crack so I could use and release myself from what ailed me. No longer was I concerned about asking for forgiveness. Certain events make an addict stressed and eager, and when their anxiety is high, so is the possibility that they'll wish for drugs again. Fear can also trigger the desire for drugs.

Then I went out to find the "evil stuff," and it wasn't so easy to get. I didn't even know where to go, but I was somewhere close to home when I found the drugs. It was not the good stuff, but it served its purpose. And I used it there—inhaled the crap—and all felt better. My breaths fled; I was floating away. I was free; I was really free.

That was the sensation, just the sensation. It was not freedom. I mean it.

Time passed, and the effect went away with time. I started thinking about my father and how I should make the apology. But now I had another problem. I had gone out and used crack. What would I say to my mother about it? I had been on the street, I think, for about three hours now. My mom would want to know how I could have done this. I had promised not to leave the house. Where was my promise of no further use? Where?

Man, it is not easy to leave this world of drugs—this parallel world. It is a very difficult thing, and it requires a tremendous amount of inner strength. I remembered a time when I met a guy who had left the drugs, and he always said it was easy to leave; you only needed determination. Where was mine now?

Time was passing, and if there is something that does not forgive, that something is the time, is not it?

I did not know what to do. But something happened just then. I had a strong urge to go back to the bushes where I'd first started using. You remember? The spot where my fellows and I had gathered together to use. It was an ugly, dirty place, and it smelled bad. But it did not matter at all.

Because I was close to home and school, I arrived promptly. I went to the spot where I had sat so often. I remembered many things that had happened there. I thought about my life and how everything would be different if I had not attended those "meetings" of Antonio's.

I sat and cried. I cried for my mother, I cried for my father, and I cried for myself. I cried for my weakness.

I cried a lot, and in the midst of my tears, I found myself praying. I prayed to God, offering my lamentations and asking for strength in order to find the strong support I would need to get up again and to be able to do what I had to do. I prayed that I would be able to ask forgiveness from Dad and start my treatment at the clinic Mr. Peter had recommended.

Well, prayer is really a balsam. If you are among those who do not pray, please start doing so soon. You will feel better. You'll be much calmer. Prayer can help you in many things, especially in moments of decision in your life. Do not lose any more time.

And that was when I gained a kind of courage and went back home.

I knocked on the door because, by then, I no longer had a house key. My mother came and opened the door immediately, without a word. I saw my father in the room and said to myself, *Now is the time to use what you asked God.*

I stood in front of my father. I was shaking inside and out. I knelt down and said," Father, I know I should not even be here in front of you, but I am your son. I messed up very, very badly. I even asked God for strength to do so. Now, I ask forgiveness for everything I did, for all your suffering, worry, hopelessness, pain, and spending." I mentioned so much I cannot remember all now.

"And, father," I continued, "please don't forsake me. You know, Dad, this world of drugs has many things that hurt inside, but your silence hurts more. Not being able to talk to you is horrible. Forgive me, please. If I have your forgiveness, I think starting over will be easier for me."

I no longer knew what to say, but I think I said all that I had in my heart.

Dad remained silent. He stood up, pulled me up by the hand, and gave me the hug that he had never given me. And for the first time in my life, I was *safe*. For the first time in a long time my happiness was back. Sure, that was not the first hug in my life, but I was truly convinced that it was utterly important.

And it was there that I think I excelled. A small phrase formed on my lips—one I had never said to him. "I love you," I said.

Saying I love you was necessary, for my father broke into tears, and it seemed that everything was going to be fine. My mother, needless to say, was in tears over that unforgettable scene.

And really it was unforgettable. I had said the right thing after all. I would seek the clinic the next day in order to start the treatment process there too.

But deep down, what I wanted was a remedy that would help me feel better and keep me from craving crack. Oh yes, that would be great. I wanted a medicine that could make me feel no desire to do drugs—something that could cut it out of me.

Outpatient

The same night, I had an urge to make an inventory of my life, of the things I'd learned during those two admissions to the clinics.

I was already an adult, nearly twenty-two years old, and I had already done a lot of craziness.

I took a pencil and paper, and as I did not want anything, I started writing. I wrote down all the experiences I'd had in life. I wrote about the drugs, made comparisons between my life before and after drugs, and analyzed what had happened to me. I wrote everything I had done to consume—the follies, the thefts, the lies, and the pain I'd felt. I put everything on paper, and as I wrote, I saw that I had done absurd things and escaped death I don't know how many times. This led me to believe that God had a plan. I had a mission, and I could better my life.

It was January, the year that I was to turn twenty-two. I continued writing. Sometimes I felt tears running down my face. My heart was heavy heart, and everything I wrote seemed like a farewell. This was what I wanted, a farewell to drugs.

It was a farewell in the form of a report of all that I had done, the amount of suffering I had caused Dad and Mom, my own suffering, and the encounter I'd had with the "guy down there." I even wrote about the best experience—my encounter with Jesus, which I'd liked very much.

I decided to write without stopping, without blinking. I wasn't concerned with sleep. What I wanted was to write a book. I wasn't sure exactly what the finished product would be. But I really wanted to write and say what was inside me, what my heart let me say.

It would be good for somebody, I thought.

For a long time that night I found myself writing and praying. I seemed to be settling into a new life.

Or was this the madness of a junkie?" The process was good. As I wrote, I relived some bad moments of my life, my seven years of living death.

Day came; the birds sang, and the cock of the house there woke up everybody. With paper and pencil, I continued without stopping. I'd had no sleep and felt no fatigue. I just wrote. All I wanted was to report what had happened. It could be a letter to my parents or a book. I did not know, but I wrote.

I had never had the courage to tell my parents what had happened to me, and in this writings they could find the details of my life in relation to drugs. I wrote about what I'd done, felt, and suffered and about the times I'd deceived people. I wrote of the days I had thought about God and hoped for His help, along with the moments I had dreamed of the devil. I recorded everything.

People think drug users don't suffer when they want to leave that life; I assure you that we do suffer a lot.

So these letters were filled up with real feelings. I talked about my fear, my desires, my meetings, and my holy encountering with Jesus.

I said everything. I did not forget. The night had passed and so I came out of my room at noon. But it was not that half day like I'd described at the beginning of my story. I hadn't woken up after a night of revelry. I would use the day differently; it would be a day of production.

I had spent twelve hours writing—writing about my life and the seven years of suffering and pain.

Wasn't seven the number that Jesus used to symbolize something in the Bible?

I thought so. I would ask my dad later, but I thought it was. And perhaps it had more meaning in my life. I believed that really was a mission that God had in store for me.

I was inclined to go to the clinic, and I got everything ready to reinvent myself, to recreate my life. I would begin anew, as Jesus once said. I believed that I had found my spirituality that night. I did not know exactly what, but something had opened up in me.

Time is a quiet miracle worker. There are forces at work that attempt to destroy everything God wants to do among us. I had a dream, a spiritual talk with Jesus.

I arranged the papers I had written—my inventory, which looked more like a life, a book. I tidied them up and put them on my bed. My intention was that my mother would see them; she would read them and see my conviction to change. I wanted to change. I wanted a new life.

As I exited the room on the way to the clinic to see how it worked, I looked back. I looked at the pile of paper on my bed. It seemed that I had written a book—a true story of a discolored *life*.

I turned and left the room. I talked with Mom and Dad. Both were bright, and Mom's eyes were radiant. The home environment had completely changed, thank God.

And I realized I was putting a little more God in my life.

Deep down, I felt anguish, but I did not know what it was.

I talked to my parents and said I would eat something quickly. After having lunch, I would go straight to the clinic to speak with the professionals there so I could start this new process.

I ate, and kissed my mother and my father. I asked Mom to look at the material I'd left on my bed. I thought that maybe, by the time I came back home, she would had read my story and we could talk. Then I left the house and headed toward the clinic.

You know, I really wanted to say all I had written out loud, but I was not courageous enough to do so. I was eager to say it all, but writing seemed like the best way to tell my parents what I needed to say. So I wrote.

I thought this new step in my life would be a page that I could write later, another page of my life.

No Time

On the way to the outpatient clinic, to my unfortunate surprise, I felt a sharp pain in the back, behind my lungs. The pain was impressive in its strength.

I fell to the ground, unable to breathe. I looked at the sky and thought, *Will this be my end?*

God waited until I had written it all to my parents, with some intention to serve for some purpose. What would it be?

I passed out for a second time within the past seven years.

When I woke up, I found myself in a hospital, this one better than the first emergency room I'd been in. A tube had been inserted into my trachea to help me breathe. As usual, my mother was beside me, and this time, my father was comforting me also.

My mother had taken my writing to the hospital. When I saw them, I got emotional and I wondered why she had brought them here. But she had not brought them with her when she'd first come to the hospital.

Dad and Mom had already spoken with the doctor, and my case was very serious. I would not get out alive. That was when she'd returned home in tears and grabbed my writing.

The doctor, this one much friendlier than the other one who had attended to me in the last emergency room, entered the room and told me the "truth." But I felt ready, ready to face what was happening. I looked at my mother, who told me that she had brought my papers because of this sad news. She wanted to congratulate me for everything, for all I had lived through and for asking my father for his forgiveness.

It was then that I asked the doctor, "Doctor how many days, how much time do I have?"

"I am not God," he replied. "But any time you have bleeding in the lungs, the situation is very dangerous. You could die any time."

You know, the word *die* did not look ugly at this time. It seemed very liberating, and so I hoped escaping this world would be.

I embraced my dear mother and lay against her. I hugged and comforted her and embraced my dad also. I said that I loved them very much and, once again, asked their forgiveness. I wanted to go to the other side empty, smooth, and free. Indeed, I was eager to go. I did not know why. I believed that God was comforting me through Jesus.

I looked at Mom and her red eyes. Life is funny. A few minutes ago, she was happy, and now she was sad.

I asked her for my papers. I also asked for a clipboard because I wanted to write more. I wanted to make sense of what had happened. I remembered all of my life again, but I had already written much about it; I had spoken of my becoming bitterly entwined in drugs and about the crack that had devastated me. I was dying. What more was there to say?

It was then that something came to my mind. I wrote about my last minutes with my parents there with me.

I saw before me the opportunity God had given me to write. And if I had not taken advantage of it, these twelve hours of writing wouldn't exist. I could now write a brief message, symbolizing the inventory of my life at its end—my dying. I wrote:

> Enjoy living next to those you love. Take time to think about what makes you say you love the people you love. *Believe in God.* Fight and be happy. Stay away from drugs. If you want to be happy, be happy now. Do not let seven years of your life pass before you begin your pursuit of happiness because, by then, it may be too late to live it with those you love.

I sincerely hope that my last statement will serve my friends, both men and women, who are still in the lanes and alleys and under the houses and huts of the various Antonios, Carloses, and Marcoses who are out there trying to provide a living death to all those who dare to unwittingly go the way of the curse of drugs.

Unexpectedly, a letter from an unknown author that I had once read came to my mind. It had been written on a piece of old paper and dropped on the floor of my school. It was a moving farewell letter from a nineteen-year-old boy addressed to his father. The boy was hospitalized, and he accurately predicted his own death. Soon after he wrote the letter, he died. It is worth disclosing the meaningful content of this letter.

Here is that last letter from a young junkie:

I do not know how my father will receive this, but I need to finally tell my story while I still can.

Sorry, Dad, I think this dialogue is the last I'll have with you. I'm really sorry. You know, Dad, it's time you know the truth that you never suspected. I'll be brief and clear. That is my very goal.

The poison killed me. I became acquainted with my killer at fifteen years of age. Is it not horrible, Father? You know how I knew this disgrace? Through a citizen who was elegantly dressed and well spoken. This citizen introduced me to my future killer—the drugs.

I tried to refuse. I tried, but the citizen messed with my pride, saying I was not a man.

I don't need to say any more, do I, Dad? I entered the world of addiction. In the beginning was the dream, and then the torture, the darkness. I did nothing without the toxic presence of drugs.

Then came the shortness of breath, the fear, and the hallucinations. And soon after, I'd experience the euphoria of the "peak" again, and I'd feel more important than other people. The toxin, my inseparable friend, made me smile and smile.

You know, my father, you start to think everything is ridiculous and very funny. Even God I found comical.

Today, in a hospital bed, I recognize that God is more important than everyone. And without his help, I would not be writing this letter.

Dad, I'm only nineteen, and I know I have no chance to live. It's too late for me. But to you, my father, I have my last request. Show this letter to all the young people that you know. Tell them that in each gate school, each prep school, and among each faculty anywhere, there's always an elegantly dressed, well-spoken man who will show them their future murderer and destroyer of their lives and who will lead them to madness and death, as happened to me. Please do this, my father, before it is too late for them.

Forgive me, Father. I already suffered too much. Forgive me for causing you to also suffer for my follies. Goodbye, my father.

Your dear son

And when I finished, I noticed this letter was like my life too . . .

*   *   *

And Paul could not keep on writing. At this point, I, his mother, am writing, continuing this beautiful testimonial that my son began as a sign and warning for the thousands of sons and daughters around the world, who are currently suffering and causing the people in their life who they love to suffer.

My son, my darling, my Paul, died of acute pulmonary emphysema. He had already contracted AIDS. He did not know this, and we never told him.

He is gone, but his legacy is here. And you can read it, pass it along, and prevent your child or your neighbor or your friend from afar from getting into drugs.

My son did not sign the story he wrote about his life, and I now do it for him, in tears, but hopeful that it—this *notice of life*—reaches thousands of homes around the world.

My Boy went to meet Jesus. May God bless you, my son. Go in peace.

Your Mama.

Alert to Parents

What are the warning signs of which parents should be aware?

Drug users are masters at lying, simulating, and manipulating. They may use drugs for a long time without their parents realizing.

Usually parents are the last to know. There are many ways to cover up the drug use.

Start watching the eyes of your sons and daughters to see if they are red. The big warning signs are changes in behavior. These include a change of friends or classmates (be especially aware of new friends who are not presented to the family); irritability; loss of appetite or compulsive, excessive eating; profound changes in the rhythm of sleep; an exchange of night for day; changes in manner of dress, often with clothes being stolen (a user may be exchanging clothes for drugs); objects that strangely disappear from home (it's probably not the employee); drastic changes in school performance (up or down); isolation; lack of care for the body; inexplicable loss of employment; absences; and constant lies, even if they are small and seemingly unimportant.

Is it possible for a user to recover, even if he or she has been using drugs for a long time?

No doubt, it is possible, as long as he or she wants and gets appropriate help. Do not forget that there will possibly be irreparable injury. This will be a reality with which the ex-addict, as well as his or her guardian, will have to live.

Then will the user never be like he or she was before the addiction?

He or she will not. The recovering addict will not be the same as before the drug. He or she will be a new human being.

Why does the addict always behave immaturely?

Because he or she is an immature person. An addict's emotional being and psyche are paralyzed as soon as he or she begins to use drugs.

"An adult is someone who has the ability to take the reins in the hands of the meaning of life." (Rudolf Steiner)

Do authoritarian parents hinder the healthy development of children?

Yes it's true. But we always mistake authoritarian parents and parents with authority.

What is codependency?

The figure of the codependent is embodied by those who live with or care for the dependent. Codependents are affected by the difficulty experienced by the dependent, and the suffering may be even higher. There are cases where the abuser does not know what he or she did, but the codependent, who is most often a family member, often has to answer for his or her actions.

However, there are those who take advantage of this suffering and lack of know-how by the codependents. I remember a very special moment when we received an AA member in our support group. He said, "The greatest enemy of the alcoholic user is his wife."

Surprised at the statement, I plied him with questions In summary, he said, "When the husband is an alcoholic, the wife is a holy martyr, the one who receives all the praise possible from relatives and acquaintances, for her patience, for her suffering, for her humiliations, and on and on.

"As the husband is useless, it is the wife who makes the decisions, who has the power in the family. When he stops using alcohol, the situation is reversed. It is he who becomes the hero, who happens to be praised by family and friends because he overcame his addiction.

"From that moment, the woman will have to at least share power in the family. Her condition as a saint ceases to exist, and she cannot adapt to the new situation. Thus, she unconsciously works toward her husband's relapse."

Many families depend on a drug addict in their midst to be happy. He is the "antenna" for all the evils that would occur. Imagine if he gets well?! People will have to look at themselves, the family will have to look at itself, and the wrong things cannot be thrown on the shoulders of drugs.

WHAT YOU SHOULD TAKE INTO CONSIDERATION

1. We have to *"teach thinking."*
2. Prior to educating our children and teenagers, we need to educate their teachers and parents.
3. The prevention of drug use has much to do with self-esteem and affection.
4. There's no point or age at which to start a prevention project; if we do not initiate communication first, drugs dealer will do so.
5. Work first with direction, guidance, and supervision. The second step involves the faculty and staff. As a third step, work with parents. Finally, the team is prepared to work with the student.
6. If the family and the school do not "speak the same language," the work of prevention will be threatened.
7. It is very important to develop critical thinking in the student and educator, to mix and create new expectations.
8. The young have much yet to learn, before or instead of learning to use drugs.
9. Let us remember that, older people can always teach us; they possess a wealth of life experience and culture.

10. We cannot speak of the drug, if we don't first talk about the value of *life*.

11. Beware of the lies of a sick society!

12. If you cannot talk or respond, someone will be waiting for the opportunity to give the answer that neither you nor the parents want to hear!

13. The best prevention is the love, affection, and dialogue that must exist in the family and school.

14. Inside the mind and heart of the child/student, there is a deluge of wishes and safe values to be cultivated.

15. The family or school that does not cultivate values is digging the grave in which to bury the happiness of its members.

16. Locking a child up is to create a fugitive. Leaving a child in full freedom is a recipe for total disaster.

17. A child/student is like a kite. Loosen the wire in a favorable wind and hold from time to time. Only then will he or she go up in life!

18. Unless you are the model of consistency, everything you say will be empty and reason for disbelief.

19. The good educator uses dialogue, knows the subject matter, has a critical sense, is the model of what he or she is preaching, acts with love and firmness, and is supportive of the user's self-esteem and values. He or she rescues the addict by keeping busy and living with love, dedication, and dialogue.

TIPS FOR HAVING CONSCIOUS ATTITUDES REGARDING DRUGS

- *Talk to your kids about alcohol and other drugs.* This may help you change their belief that drinking alcohol, smoking, and using other drugs is normal and accepted.
- *Listen carefully to your children.* They will share their experiences with you. Show interest and listen to them attentively and actively during every moment of their speech.
- *Help your children feel good.* Your children will feel good when you praise their efforts and achievements. Strengthen their self-esteem and criticize their actions and not them as people.
- *Help your children develop proper, firm values.* If your children have adequate, firm values, they will be strong and full of certainty and be able to say *no* to alcohol, tobacco, and other drugs. They will not be left following what their friends says.

- *Always be a good example!* Habits and customs that you have when it comes to the consumption of alcohol, tobacco, and other drugs strongly influence the ideas that your children will have in relation to this consumption.

- *Look for positive comparisons.* Relate to your children success stories and attitudes of affirmation in the face of life's difficulties.

- *Help your children overcome peer pressure.* Children who live with respect, affection, and security and who have high self-esteem are much more likely to handle the pressure of groups of friends with a firm *no* to drugs and positive attitude toward a drug-free life.

- *Establish family rules.* Establish specific and clear rules about drug use and the type of discipline that a family member who engages with them will receive.

- *Encourage and create healthy activities.* Leisure activities, such as extracurricular school events, religious activities, sports, and social events help your children combat idleness and prevent drug abuse.

User, if you lack the strength to confront your addiction, seek advice from professionals and trust your heart to that which was and remains the greatest psychotherapist of all time—Jesus Christ. Your attendance is free; just get him through prayer.

Psalm 23 (ESV Bible)

The LORD is my shepherd; I shall not want.

He makes me lie down in green pastures.

He leads me beside still waters.

He restores my soul.

He leads me in paths of righteousness for his name's sake.

Even though I walk through the valley of the shadow of death, I will fear no evil, for you are with me; your rod and your staff, they comfort me.

You prepare a table before me in the presence of my enemies; you anoint my head with oil; my cup overflows.

Surely goodness and mercy shall follow me all the days of my life, and I shall dwell in the house of the LORD forever.

*   *   *

Hebrews 6:11-12

And we desire each one of you to show the same earnestness to have the full assurance of hope until the end.

So that you may not be sluggish, but imitators of those who through faith and patience inherit the promises.

About the Author

Aluney Elferr Albuquerque Silva is a writer, speaker, theologian, clinical psychoanalyst, and master and doctor of theology and psychoanalysis. He entered the Brazilian Association of Psychosomatic Medicine and Federal District Council Federation of Theology. He is a motivational speaker and consultant with training in neurolinguistic programming (NLP), a prevention consultant, and a consultant in chemical dependency. He completed graduate university as an extension advisor on drugs and faith in prevention, both from the Universidade Federal de Santa Catarina (UFSC).

He is a drug therapist, a holistic therapist, and a therapist in the flower of Bach. He is vice president of the Brazilian Association of Parents of Drug Users, former president of the Municipal Anti-Drug Council of Manaus, former vice chairman of the municipal anti-drug Manacapuru, and national president of the National Union of Advisers on Drugs. In addition, he is a researcher with the Research Network of the National Drug Policy on Drugs and is dedicated to the study of human behavior. He is president and founder of the Institute NAF Brazil.

He is the author of the following books:

Drugs: The Parallel Universe

Drugs: The Climb

I Owner of Myself: Face Challenges

Unconscious Mental Processes

At the Time of Pain